A Twelve-Session Unit

Nuclear War
Teaching Manual for
The Challenge of Peace

Brother Stephen Markham, FSC

Faith and Justice Issues 3
Saint Mary's Press
Christian Brothers Publications
Winona, Minnesota

Consulting editors: Stephan Nagel; Robert Smith, FSC; Rev. Robert
              Stamschror; Thomas Zanzig.

Cover photo by Technicolor Government Services, Inc.
Line drawings by Carolyn Thomas.

Excerpts from *The Challenge of Peace: God's Promise and Our Response*
copyright © 1983 by the United States Catholic Conference. All rights re-
served. A copy of the complete pastoral letter may be ordered from the Office of Publishing Services, U.S.C.C., 1312 Massachusetts Avenue, N.W.,
Washington, D.C. 20005.

Scriptural excerpts used in this work are taken from The Jerusalem Bible,
published and copyright 1966, 1967 and 1968 by Darton, Longman and Todd
Limited and Doubleday & Co. Inc., and are used by permission of the
publishers.

ISBN: 0-88489-156-9

Contents

Introduction

During the past twenty years great efforts have been made to include peace studies in high school and college curricula. In some cases complete courses on issues of justice and peace have been added to the regular curriculum. In other cases mini-units on peace issues have been incorporated within courses already existing.

The National Conference of Catholic Bishops (NCCB), under the leadership of Archbishop John R. Roach of the Archdiocese of St. Paul and Minneapolis, has made a great contribution to the cause of peace and to the inclusion of peace studies in educational programs throughout the country with the publication of its pastoral letter, *The Challenge of Peace: God's Promise and Our Response.*

This unit is intended to help senior high school students study the bishops' pastoral letter. There are twelve sessions offered in this manual. Additional or alternative class activities are included at the end of several of the sessions. Several activities suggested for students in this unit will be most effective if each student has a copy of the activity. These activities are included within the text of the manual at the end of each respective session—thus easily available for duplication purposes. Also included is an appendix designed as a study guide for adult discussion or seminar groups.

The twelve session plans can be used as a unit within a regular high school curriculum or as part of a parish CCD or seminar program. The study guide can be used for faculty in-service programs or with other adult groups connected with high school or parish religious education programs.

The complete text of the bishops' pastoral letter is available through:

Office of Publishing Services
United States Catholic Conference
1312 Massachusetts Avenue, NW
Washington, D.C. 20005
Phone: 202-659-6785
Publication no. 863

The cost per copy is $1.00 plus postage and handling charges. Payment must be included with all orders of twenty-five or fewer copies. Postage and handling charges are as follows:

1 to 10 copies	—	$1.25
11 to 25 copies	—	$2.50
26 to 50 copies	—	$4.00
51 to 100 copies	—	$5.00

Note: You will need copies of the pastoral itself for your students or discussion group since the twelve session plans and the study guide provided in this manual are intended to be used with the text of the letter.

The following is a **brief summary** of the twelve sessions included in this manual: *Session 1* introduces the unit, giving the students an overview of what will be taught and engaging them in discussing why the bishops have written this pastoral letter. *Session 2* invites the students to share their own perceptions of the "signs of the times" in regard to nuclear disarmament. *Session 3* addresses the Church's role in matters of peace and war, identifying the "signs of the times" expressed by the Catholic bishops of the United States and pointing out reasons why the bishops have written this pastoral letter to the Catholic community as well as to the wider political community. *Session 4* sets forth the scriptural basis for peace, recognizing that peace is a gift from God and is attained through reconciliation and expressed in love. In *session 5* the students have a chance to share their own views on the possibility of peace in the world today and to learn of the bishops' conviction that peace is possible.

Session 6 addresses the Christian perspective of the just-war theory and encourages the students to reflect on the pacifist option and nonviolent tradition. In *session 7* the bishops' stand on the issue of nuclear weapons is clearly stated, and the moral issues surrounding the question of nuclear warfare are addressed. *Session 8* challenges the students to discuss and debate the moral dimensions of nuclear deterrence and to identify what the bishops are saying about the issue. *Session 9* introduces the students to the specific steps proposed by the bishops that are aimed at a more adequate policy for preserving peace in a nuclear age. Session 9 also asks the students to think of ways in which they can contribute to reducing the danger of war. *Session 10* raises the question of interdependence among nations that are facing the problems of meeting both security and welfare needs. *Session 11* provides options for individual and group actions intended to help create a world of peace and understanding. *Session 12* allows the students to review, react to, and express their reponses to the challenges the bishops are presenting to them in this pastoral letter.

Overall Goals and Rationale for Teaching This Unit

Teaching Goal: To help the students recognize and consider the moral dimensions of a world arming itself with nuclear weapons.

Behavioral Goal: For the students to learn what the Catholic bishops of the United States have said in their pastoral letter, *The Challenge of Peace: God's Promise and Our Response.*

Rationale: The bishops speak out!

The faith that Jesus is Lord begins with each of us individually and has to consume the Church—otherwise we are not going to be peacemakers. (Bishop Raymond Hunthausen of Seattle)

I would insist that anyone who is going to follow the nonviolent words of Christ will have to go through a spiritual conversion. (Bishop Thomas Gumbleton of Detroit)

Nuclear weapons are immoral, and if that's true, then it's immoral for us to build, assemble, deploy, and threaten to use them. (Bishop Leroy Matthiesen of Amarillo, Texas)

The issue is not simply political. The Church must be a participant in protecting the world and its people from the specter of nuclear destruction. (Cardinal Joseph Louis Bernardin of Chicago)

The Church's teaching on nuclear weapons is the best kept secret in the world. (Bishop Walter Sullivan of Richmond, Virginia)

This secret is not so well kept anymore. In November 1981, Archbishop John Roach, president of the National Conference of Catholic Bishops, said to the conference in his opening address: "On a global scale, the most dangerous moral issue in the public order today is the nuclear arms race. . . . The Church needs to say no clearly and decisively to the use of nuclear arms." He called the bishops to leadership in efforts to stop the arms race.

The bishops of the United States Catholic Church have taken their president's call seriously. In June 1982, the bishops spent eleven days together at Collegeville, Minnesota, where they discussed their roles and responsibilities as spiritual and pastoral leaders in the Catholic Church. At this gathering the bishops received copies of the first official draft of the document which would eventually become the pastoral letter: *The Challenge of Peace: God's Promise and Our Response.* This original draft has been revised three

times since June 1982 and is now endorsed and published as an official statement of the National Conference of Catholic Bishops:

Our God speaks and calls us to listen. Throughout history God's people have sought to hear and to respond. They have done so in ways marked by human frailty, yet guided by the Spirit. Today as never before we are called to listen to God's word as it speaks in our world and in our nation.

These opening remarks from the original draft of the bishops' document, published in the *National Catholic Reporter,* 2 July 1982, express well what the bishops have set out to do, what we are asked to do, and what we are striving to foster in the lives of the youth we teach.

It is particularly appropriate to teach seventeen-, eighteen-, or nineteen-year-olds what the Catholic bishops are saying on matters such as the challenge of peace. During these latter teenage years young people often make major lifestyle and career decisions that will affect their futures. Topics that influence and directly affect the options available to them—and the moral dilemmas facing them—are of great interest and concern to this age group. Furthermore, for many Catholics, it is during these latter teenage years that they all too frequently participate in their last "formal" or "official" religious education program in high school or parish. Perhaps a serious study at this time of what the bishops are teaching on a topic so pertinent to their lives will foster an openness among these young people and, in years to come, they may look forward to and seek out insights from their bishops and their Church as they strive to grow in faith—aided primarily by their own experiences and their involvement in parish life.

Planning the Individual Sessions

Each of the twelve sessions in this manual is complete with an assignment, an overall teaching goal, a session objective formed specifically for the session being taught, a classroom activity described in detail, and summary points. Your most practical and specific planning for teaching this unit will involve designing or adapting the session plans to meet the needs of your students. The following section offers definitions of the component parts of each session.

Teaching Goal: The teaching goal is a specific goal for each session that is subordinate to the overall teaching goal for the unit. Therefore, choose or create a teaching goal for each session that will help to achieve the more general goal of the course as a whole. This session goal, to be consistent with your unique setting and circumstances, should be as concrete and specific as possible. It is often helpful to share with the students the teaching goal for an individual session.

Session Objective: The session objective is a behavioral objective formed specifically for the session being taught. It should be one that can be reasonably attained, is considerate of your students' background and experience, and is consistent with the teaching goal for the session. Session objectives should not be overambitious. For example, if your teaching goal is to help students keep alive the conviction and the hope that peace is possible, your session objective should not be "for *all* students to witness to *all* whom they meet the conviction that peace is possible." Rather, the objective could be "for the students to identify the conviction that peace is possible as expressed by the National Conference of Catholic Bishops in their pastoral letter." Attempt to keep the session objective simple and clear.

The author of this manual has stated an objective for each of the sessions. The class activities suggested for each session are designed with this objective in mind, but it is important for you to revise or rewrite the session objectives in your own words, adapting them to your students or group and making each one express just what you want to do in the session. You will then choose or adapt classroom activities to accomplish your own session objectives.

Class Activity: Choose, adapt, or create activities that will help you accomplish your session objective and that are appropriate for your particular setting and circumstances. Before presenting or undertaking any activity or experience, know what you plan to do, how you plan to do it, and why you are doing it. This preparation is particularly necessary when you are us-

ing activities suggested in this manual since it is important that you make them your own and adapt them to fit your session objectives.

Summary: Allow a few minutes for summary—a brief time to make connections, stress particular points or happenings in the session, reclarify the purpose of the session, and affirm the students—at the end of each session. This is an appropriate time to refer the students to additional resources or experiences, and/or it can be an opportunity for you to share a personal experience that helps to complete the session.

Assignment: Choose, adapt, or create activities appropriate for your group and circumstances. The assignment is often a reflection or assimilation activity, but it may also be an experience that initiates the learning process. The nature of the assignment will differ depending on its purpose: to facilitate reflection or evaluation of what has been learned or to introduce the student to what is to be covered in a later session. *Note:* Many of the assignments suggested for the twelve sessions in this manual could be adapted to serve as classroom activities.

Note: It is important to review your entire session plan several days beforehand and to see that you have all the needed materials. It is also wise to check the availability and working order of any needed audiovisual equipment at least one day before beginning the session. Very likely, you will have established a pattern or system for dealing with routine preliminaries (seating arrangement, attendance check, review of previous session, return of papers, prayer). In some sessions prayer might fit well during the group activity or the summary. The actual prayer form (individual, group, responsorial, chant, silent, and so on), as well as the time it occurs, might well be varied from session to session. When you review your session plans make special note of any needs or preliminary preparations that are unique to the particular session.

Session 1
Purpose and Overview

Teaching Goal: To introduce this unit, *Nuclear War: Teaching Manual for* **The Challenge of Peace.**

Session Objective: To give the students an overview of the unit and to help them identify the reasons the bishops state for writing the pastoral letter entitled *The Challenge of Peace: God's Promise and Our Response.*

Revised Objective:

Class Activities:

1) Give the students an overview of the unit. The preceding introductory pages of this manual can provide you with information for this introductory overview. (10 minutes)

2) Ask a student to read aloud the introduction (nos. 1–4) of *The Challenge of Peace.*

Then, review the material read and write on the board the reasons the bishops give for publishing this pastoral letter:

- *We agree that the world is at a moment of crisis.*
- *It is . . . our intent . . . to speak words of hope and encouragement in time of fear.*
- *We wish to provide hope and strength to all who seek a world free of the nuclear threat.*

Discuss with the students: Why do the bishops believe the world is at a moment of crisis? Do you agree?

What do you think the bishops might say that would give you hope or encouragement? Why do the bishops believe that hope is feasible in this time of supreme crisis and fear? (20–30 minutes)

Summary: Highlight key points from the session. Emphasize the bishops' definition of hope (see no. 2): (a) "Hope sustains one's capacity to live with danger without being overwhelmed by it." (b) ". . . hope is the will to struggle against obstacles even when they appear insuperable." (c) ". . . our hope rests in the God who gave us life, sustains the world by his power, and has called us to revere the lives of every person and all peoples." (10 minutes)

Session 2
Signs of the Times

Assignment: Ask each student to find two newspaper articles on the nuclear disarmament issue. Have the students read the articles and answer the following questions for each of them. (*Note:* Ask the students to bring these written responses as well as their two articles to class.)

1) What stand regarding nuclear disarmanent does this article promote?
   _____ strongly in favor of nuclear disarmament
   _____ rather neutral or noncommittal
   _____ strongly opposed to nuclear disarmament
2) What is your response to this article?
   _____ strongly agree
   _____ neutral or noncommittal
   _____ strongly disagree
3) What question would you like to ask the author of this article?

(*Note:* This assignment activity is available, in format for duplication, at the end of this session.)

Teaching Goal: To help the students be aware of the "signs of the times" relative to peace and war in the world.

Session Objective: For the students to share their own perceptions of the "signs of the times" in regard to the issue of nuclear disarmament.

Revised Objective:

Class Activities:

1) On the chalkboard write:

Nuclear Disarmament

Article survey		Student survey
	strongly in favor of	
_____		_____
	neutral or noncommittal	
_____		_____
	strongly opposed to	
_____		_____

Now, indicate the total number of articles that the students found for their assignment that are "strongly in favor of" nuclear disarmament. You might determine this number by having each student raise one hand if one of his or her articles is in favor of nuclear disarmament, or raise both hands if both of the articles he or she found are in favor of nuclear disarmament.

Repeat this process to determine the number of articles the students found for their assignment that are "neutral" and the number that are "opposed" to nuclear disarmament.

Use the same process to determine the number of students in the class who strongly agree, are neutral, or strongly disagree with the articles they read.

Now reflect for a minute with the class on the results of the survey as recorded. Ask for student observations and then share your own comments on the commonality or diversity of views presented by the articles or expressed by the group. (15 minutes)

2) Ask the students to share some of the questions they would like to ask the authors of the articles which they read for the assignment above. Invite the students to interact and discuss their own views regarding some of these questions. When you have a sense of where the students stand on this topic, bring the discussion to closure by sharing your impression of where the group seems to be. For example: "We seem to recognize how complex this issue is" or "We seem to be very enthusiastic (confused, whatever) about this issue." (20 minutes)

Summary: Commend the students for their involvement and point out that the main point of this unit is to study what the National Conference of Catholic Bishops is saying in its pastoral letter, *The Challenge of Peace: God's Promise and Our Response.* Ask the students to pin on the bulletin board the newspaper articles from their assignment along with the question they raised for each author. This visual display in the classroom can serve as a reminder to the students of the importance and complexity of the unanswered questions involved in the issues surrounding nuclear disarmament. If time permits, allow the students to move about the room reading articles found or questions raised by other students. (15 minutes)

NEWSPAPER ARTICLE STUDY

Find two newspaper articles on the nuclear disarmament issue. Read the two articles and answer the following questions for each of them. (*Note:* Bring these written responses as well as the two articles to class.)

1. What stand regarding nuclear disarmament does this article promote?

   _____ strongly in favor of nuclear disarmament

   _____ rather neutral or noncommittal

   _____ strongly opposed to nuclear disarmament

2. What is your response to this article?

   _____ strongly agree

   _____ neutral or noncommittal

   _____ strongly disagree

3. What question would you like to ask the author of this article?

Session 3
Religious Perspectives, Pastoral Responsibilities, and Political Realities

Assignment: Ask the students to read the next section of the bishops' pastoral letter (nos. 5–26), which focuses on the bishops' purpose for writing the letter and offers orientation and background for understanding the bishops' position. Then have the students complete the exercise "Why Did the Bishops Write *The Challenge of Peace*?" (*Note:* This exercise is available, in format for duplication, at the end of this session.)

Teaching Goal: To help the students understand the Church's role in teaching on matters of peace and war.

Session Objective: For the students to identify reasons why the bishops wrote this pastoral letter to the Catholic community as well as to the wider political community.

Revised Objective:

Class Activities:

1) Review from the previous session those "signs of the times" which the students highlighted as ones which are reflected in their own lives.
On the board write:
The Signs of the Times
a) The world wants peace. The world needs peace.
b) The arms race is a curse inflicting harm on the poor.
c) Nuclear arms present new problems for traditional moral principles.

Discuss with the students how these signs of the times (a–c above) have influenced the bishops' writing of this pastoral letter. (Note no. 13 of the pastoral letter.) (15 minutes)

2) Ask the students to compare their responses to the exercise in the assignment above. Then take a survey recording the students' responses to the following:

The Catholic bishops should (please choose only *one* of the following):
_____ a) speak to Catholics in a specific way about the nuclear arms race
_____ b) speak to the wider political community in terms of public policy regarding the nuclear arms race
_____ c) both *a* and *b* above
_____ d) neither *a* nor *b* above

(*Note:* This class activity is available, in format for duplication, at the end of this session.)

Ask the students to share with the class why they chose the response they did and discuss with them: Why do the bishops themselves believe that *c* is the correct answer?
Discuss with the students: What is the distinctive role the Church has to play in the search for peace in the world today?
If it is true that "peace will be achieved fully only in the kingdom of God" (no. 20), why must we (the Church) continue to pray and work for peace? (20 minutes)

3) Have the students brainstorm a list of major issues of injustice (abortion, world hunger, ecological abuse). List these on the board and briefly note how the injustice in each issue is connected to a violation of human dignity. (10 minutes)

Summary: Highlight key points from the discussion. Invite the students to react to and discuss their response to the following statement from *The Challenge of Peace:* "The human person is the clearest reflection of God's presence in the world. . . . God is the Lord of life, and so each human life is sacred; modern warfare threatens the obliteration of human life on a previously unimaginable scale" (no. 15). (10 minutes)

WHY DID THE BISHOPS WRITE
THE CHALLENGE OF PEACE?

The three statements below are taken directly from **The Challenge of Peace: God's Promise and Our Response.** Each of the statements begins with "We believe" (emphasis added), and accordingly each expresses beliefs held in common by the bishops of the United States.

1. As bishops **we believe** that the nature of Catholic moral teaching, the principles of Catholic ecclesiology [teaching], and the demands of our pastoral ministry require that this letter speak both to Catholics in a specific way and to the wider political community regarding public policy" (no. 19).
2. "**We believe** the religious vision [of peace among peoples and nations] has an objective basis and is capable of progressive realization" (no. 20).
3. "**We believe** that the Church, as a community of faith and social institution, has a proper, necessary, and distinctive part to play in the pursuit of peace" (no. 21).

The following fifteen statements are based on **The Challenge of Peace,** and each gives some indication why the bishops wrote this pastoral letter. On the line before each statement indicate with a **1, 2,** or **3** the belief statement above that seems to correspond most directly to the statement at hand. (*Note:* There are no "right" or "wrong" answers for this exercise; it is simply for discussion purposes).

_____ a. to fulfill a pastoral responsibility (no. 5)

_____ b. to address concrete questions concerning the arms race, weapons systems, and negotiating strategies (no. 9)

_____ c. to call Catholics and all members of our political community both to dialogue and to come to specific decisions about this awesome question (no. 6)

_____ d. to bring the light of the gospel to bear upon "the signs of the times" (no. 13)

_____ e. to examine Catholic teaching on peace and war (no. 13)

_____ f. to speak to Catholics in a specific way, helping them form their consciences (no. 19)

_____ g. to speak to the wider political community in terms of public policy (no. 19)

_____ h. to contribute to the public policy debate about the morality of war (no. 16)

_____ i. to discuss the religious vision of peace among peoples and nations (no. 20)

_____ j. to undertake a completely fresh reappraisal of war (no. 23)

_____ k. to ground the task of peacemaking solidly in the biblical vision of the kingdom of God (no. 25)

_____ l. to place the task of peacemaking centrally in the ministry of the Church (no. 25)

_____ m. to specify the obstacles in the way of peace (no. 25)

_____ n. to identify the specific contributions a community of faith can make to the work of peace (no. 25)

_____ o. to offer a first step toward a message of peace and hope (no. 26)

SURVEY ON EXTENT OF COMMUNICATION ABOUT THE NUCLEAR ARMS RACE

The Catholic bishops should (please choose only **one** of the following):

_____ a. speak to Catholics in a specific way about the nuclear arms race

_____ b. speak to the wider political community in terms of public policy regarding the nuclear arms race

_____ c. both **a** and **b** above

_____ d. neither **a** nor **b** above

Session 4
Peace and the Kingdom: A Scriptural Basis

Assignment: Divide the class into two groups and ask each group to do one of the two exercises—"Old Testament Quotations" or "New Testament Quotations." (*Note:* These assignment exercises are available, in format for duplication, at the end of this session.)

Teaching Goal: To help the students discover that the roots of our search for peace lie in the Word of God as that Word is given to us in sacred Scripture.

Session Objective: For the students to identify the scriptural basis for peace as a gift from God, attained through reconciliation and expressed in love.

Revised Objective:

Class Activities:

1) Ask the students to recall times in their lives when they experienced a sense of peace. Further ask them when and why they identified that peace as a gift from God. If time permits, you could ask for volunteers to share examples, but the main purpose of this activity is for the students' personal reflection. (10 minutes)

2) Ask the students who did "Old Testament Quotations" (see assignment exercise 1 following this session) to share insights they gained from reflecting on the scriptural passages and to discuss their answers to the questions: (*a*) What is peace besides an absence of war? (*b*) If peace is a gift from God, does that mean that we do nothing? Why or why not? (*c*) Can we have peace without God? Why or why not? (20 minutes)

3) Ask the students who did "New Testament Quotations" (see assignment exercise 2 following this session) to share insights they gained from reflecting on the scriptural passages and to discuss their answers to the questions: (*a*) Which of the above passages speaks to peace between individuals? peace within families? peace within a parish or a school community? peace between nations? (*b*) How does reconciliation come about between individuals? between nations? (*c*) Is it humanly possible to love your enemies, to do good to those who hate you? Does this apply to nations? (20 minutes)

Summary: Repeat the statement from the pastoral letter: "Peace and war must always be seen in light of God's intervention in human affairs and our response to that intervention" (no. 28).

Additional or Alternative Activity:

• Assign each scriptural passage (see "Old Testament Quotations" and "New Testament Quotations" immediately following this session) to a different student. Ask three or four other students to take turns reading aloud the text of the pastoral letter (nos. 27–55). Have each student who has been assigned a scriptural passage read it aloud when it is referred to in the text.

OLD TESTAMENT QUOTATIONS

Read and reflect on the following scriptural passages and then answer, in writing, the following questions:

1. What is peace besides an absence of war?
2. If peace is a gift from God, does that mean that we do nothing? Why or why not?
3. Can we have peace without God? Why or why not?

WAR

Deuteronomy 1:30 And I said to you: Do not take fright, do not be afraid of them. Yahweh your God goes in front of you and will be fighting on your side as you saw him fight for you in Egypt.

Deuteronomy 20:4 Yahweh your God goes with you to fight for you against your enemies and to save you.

Joshua 2:24 They said to Joshua, "Yahweh has delivered the whole country into our hands, and its inhabitants all tremble already at the thought of us."

Judges 3:28 And he said to them, "Follow me, because Yahweh has delivered your enemy Moab into your hands." So they followed him, cut Moab off from crossing the fords of the Jordan and let no one across.

PEACE

Leviticus 26:12 I will live in your midst; I will be your God and you shall be my people.

Leviticus 26:3-16 If you live according to my laws, if you keep my commandments and put them into practice, I will give you the rain you need at the right time; the earth shall give its produce and the trees of the countryside their fruits; you shall thresh until vintage time and gather grapes until sowing time. You shall eat your fill of bread and live secure in your land.

I will give peace to the land, and you shall sleep with none to frighten you. I will rid the land of beasts of prey. The sword shall not pass through your land. You shall pursue your enemies and they shall fall before your sword; five of you pursuing a hundred of them, one hundred pursuing ten thousand; and your enemies shall fall before your sword.

I will turn towards you, I will make you be fruitful and multiply, and I will uphold my Covenant with you.

You shall eat your fill of last year's harvest, and still throw out the old to make room for the new.

I will set up my dwelling among you, and I will not cast you off. I will live in your midst; I will be your God and you shall be my people. It is I, Yahweh your God, who have brought you out of the land of Egypt so that you should be their servants no longer. I have broken the yoke that bound you and have made you walk with head held high.

But if you do not listen to me, and do not observe each one of these commandments, if you refuse my laws and disregard my customs, and break my Covenant by not observing each one of my commandments, then I will deal in like manner with you.

Ezekiel 37:26 I shall make a covenant of peace with them, an eternal covenant with them. I shall resettle them and increase them; I shall settle my sanctuary among them for ever.

Ezekiel 13:16 . . . these prophets of Israel who prophesy about Jerusalem and have visions of peace for her when there is no peace—it is the Lord Yahweh who speaks.

Jeremiah 6:14 They dress my people's wound without concern: "Peace! Peace!" they say, but there is no peace.

Jeremiah 8:10–12 So I will give their wives to other men, their fields to new masters, for all, least no less than greatest, all are out for dishonest gain; prophet no less than priest, all practice fraud. They dress my people's wound without concern: Peace! Peace! they say, but there is no peace. They should be ashamed of their abominable deeds. But not they! They feel no shame, they have forgotten how to blush. And so as others fall, they too shall fall; they shall be thrown down when I come to deal with them—says Yahweh.

Isaiah 7:1–9 In the reign of Ahaz son of Jotham, son of Uzziah, king of Judah, Razon the king of Aram went up against Jerusalem with Pekah son of Remaliah, king of Israel, to lay siege to it; but he was unable to capture it.

The news was brought to the House of David. "Aram," they said, "has reached Ephraim." Then the heart of the king and the hearts of the people shuddered as the trees of the forest shudder in front of the wind. Yahweh said to Isaiah, "Go with your son Shear-jashub, and meet Ahaz at the end of the conduit of the upper pool on the Fuller's Field road, and say to him: 'Pay attention, keep calm, have no fear, do not let your heart sink because of these two smouldering stumps of firebrands, or because Aram, Ephraim and the son of Remaliah have plotted to ruin you, and have said: Let us invade Judah and terrorise it and seize it for

ourselves, and set up a king there, the son of Tabeel. The Lord Yahweh says this: It shall not come true; it shall not be. The capital of Aram is Damascus, the head of Damascus, Razon; the capital of Ephraim, Samaria, the head of Samaria, the son of Remaliah. Six or five years more and a shattered Ephraim shall no longer be a people. But if you do not stand by me, you will not stand at all.' "

Isaiah 30:1-4 Woe to those rebellious sons! —it is Yahweh who speaks. They carry out plans that are not mine and make alliances not inspired by me, and so add sin to sin. They have left for Egypt, without consulting me, to take refuge in Pharaoh's protection, to shelter in Egypt's shadow. Pharaoh's protection will be your shame, the shelter of Egypt's shadow your confounding. For his ministers have gone to Zoan, his ambassadors have already reached Hanes.

Jeremiah 37:10 Even if you cut to pieces the whole Chaldaean army now fighting against you until there were only the wounded left, they would stand up again, each man in his tent, to burn this city down.

Isaiah 48:18 If only you had been alert to my commandments, your happiness would have been like a river, your integrity like the waves of the sea.

Isaiah 32:15-20 Once more there will be poured on us the spirit from above; then shall the wilderness be fertile land and fertile land become forest.

In the wilderness justice will come to live and integrity in the fertile land; integrity will bring peace, justice give lasting security.

My people will live in a peaceful home, in safe houses, in quiet dwellings—the forest shall be beaten down and the city laid low. Happy will you be, sowing by every stream, letting ox and donkey roam free.

Isaiah 2:4 He will wield authority over the nations and adjudicate between many peoples; these will hammer their swords into ploughshares, their spears into sickles. Nation will not lift sword against nation, there will be no more training for war.

Micah 4:3 He will wield authority over many peoples and arbitrate for mighty nations; they will hammer their swords into ploughshares, their spears into sickles. Nations will not lift sword against nation, there will be no more training for war.

Psalm 85:10-11 Love and Loyalty now meet, Righteousness and Peace now embrace; Loyalty reaches up from earth and Righteousness leans down from heaven.

Isaiah 42:2-3 He does not cry out or shout aloud, or make his voice heard in the streets. He does not break the crushed reed, nor quench the wavering flame.

NEW TESTAMENT QUOTATIONS

Read and reflect on the following scriptural passages and then answer, in writing, the following questions:

1. Which of the following passages speaks to
   a. peace between individuals?
   b. peace within families?
   c. peace within a parish or a school community?
   d. peace between nations?
2. How does reconciliation come about between individuals? between nations?
3. Is it humanly possible to love your enemies, to do good to those who hate you? (Luke 6:27) Does this apply to nations?

Matthew 12:18-21 *Here is my servant whom I have chosen, my beloved, the favorite of my soul. I will endow him with my spirit, and he will proclaim the true faith to the nations. He will not brawl or shout, nor will anyone hear his voice in the streets. He will not break the crushed reed, nor put out the smouldering wick till he has led the truth to victory: in his name the nations will put their hope.*

John 4:19-26 "I see you are a prophet, sir," said the woman. "Our fathers worshipped on this mountain, while you say that Jerusalem is the place where one ought to worship."

Jesus said: "Believe me, woman, the hour is coming when you will worship the Father neither on this mountain nor in Jerusalem. You worship what you do not know; we worship what we do know; for salvation comes from the Jews. But the hour will come—in fact it is here already—when true worshippers will worship the Father in spirit and truth: that is the kind of worshipper the Father wants. God is spirit, and those who worship must worship in spirit and truth."

The woman said to him, "I know that Messiah—that is, Christ—is coming; and when he comes he will tell us everything." "I who am speaking to you," said Jesus, "I am he."

Colossians 1:19-20 ... because God wanted all perfection to be found in him and all things to be reconciled through him and for him, everything in heaven and everything on earth, when he made peace by his death on the cross.

WAR

Revelation 17:14 ... and they will go to war against the Lamb; but the Lamb is *the Lord of lords and King of kings,* and he will defeat them and they will be defeated by his followers, the called, the chosen, the faithful.

Luke 14:31 Or again, what king marching to war against another king would not first sit down and consider whether with ten thousand men he could stand up to the other who advanced against him with twenty thousand?

Luke 22:35-38 He said to them, "When I sent you out without purse or haversack or sandals, were you short of anything?" "No," they said. He said to them, "But now if you have a purse, take it; if you have a haversack, do the same; if you have no sword, sell your cloak and buy one, because I tell you these words of scripture have to be fulfilled in me: *He let himself be taken for a criminal.* Yes, what scripture says about me is even now reaching its fulfilment." "Lord," they said, "there are two swords here now." He said to them, "That is enough!"

Matthew 12:34 Brood of vipers, how can your speech be good when you are evil? For a man's words flow out of what fills his heart.

Hebrews 4:12 The word of God is something alive and active: it cuts like any double-edged sword but more finely: it can slip through the place where the soul is divided from the spirit, or joints from the marrow; it can judge the secret emotions and thoughts.

Luke 22:51 But at this Jesus spoke. "Leave off!" he said. "That will do!" And touching the man's ear he healed him.

Ephesians 6:10-17 Finally, grow strong in the Lord, with the strength of his power. Put God's armour on so as to be able to resist the devil's tactics. For it is not against human enemies that we have to struggle, but against the Sovereignties and the Powers who originate the darkness in this world, the spiritual army of evil in the heavens. That is why you must rely on God's armour, or you will not be able to put up any resistance when the worst happens, or have enough resources to hold your ground.

So stand your ground, with *truth buckled around your waist,* and *integrity for a breastplate,* wearing for shoes on your feet *the eagerness to spread the gospel of peace* and always carrying the shield of faith so that you can use it to put out the burning arrows of the evil one. And then you must accept *salvation from God to be your helmet* and receive the word of God from the Spirit to use as a sword.

1 Thessalonians 5:8-9 . . . but we belong to the day and we should be sober; let us put on faith and love for a *breastplate,* and the hope of *salvation* for a *helmet.* God never meant us to experience the Retribution, but to win salvation through our Lord Jesus Christ. . . .

Matthew 8:5-13 When he went into Capernaum a centurion came up and pleaded with him. "Sir," he said, "my servant is lying at home paralysed, and in great pain." "I will come myself and cure him," said Jesus. The centurion replied, "Sir, I am not worthy to have you under my roof; just give the word and my servant will be cured. For I am under authority myself, and have soldiers under me; and I say to one man: Go, and he goes; to another: Come here, and he comes; to my servant: Do this, and he does it." When Jesus heard this he was astonished and said to those following him, "I tell you solemnly, nowhere in Israel have I found faith like this. And I tell you that many will come from east and west to take their places with Abraham and Isaac and Jacob at the feast in the kingdom of heaven; but the subjects of the kingdom will be turned out into the dark, where there will be weeping and grinding of teeth." And to the centurion Jesus said, "Go back, then; you have believed, so let this be done for you." And the servant was cured at that moment.

John 4:46-53 He went again to Cana in Galilee, where he had changed the water into wine. Now there was a court official there whose son was ill at Capernaum, and, hearing that Jesus had arrived in Galilee from Judaea, he went and asked him to come and cure his son as he was at the point of death. Jesus said, "So you will not believe unless you see signs and portents!" "Sir," answered the official, "come down before my child dies." "Go home," said Jesus, "your son will live." The man believed what Jesus had said and started on his way; and while he was still on the journey back his servants met him with the news that his boy was alive. He asked them when the boy had begun to recover. "The fever left him yesterday," they said, "at the seventh hour." The father realized that this was exactly the time when Jesus had said, "Your son will live"; and he and all his household believed.

Matthew 10:34 Do not suppose that I have come to bring peace to the earth: it is not peace I have come to bring, but a sword.

PEACE

Mark 1:15 "The time has come," he said, "and the kingdom of God is close at hand. Repent, and believe the Good News."

Matthew 4:17 From that moment, Jesus began his preaching with the message, "Repent, for the kingdom of heaven is close at hand."

Luke 17:20–21 Asked by the Pharisees when the kingdom of God was to come, he gave them this answer, "The coming of the kingdom of God does not admit to observation and there will be no one to say, 'Look here! Look there!' For, you must know, the kingdom of God is among you."

Luke 12:32 There is no need to be afraid, little flock, for it has pleased your Father to give you the kingdom.

Matthew 5:3–10 "How happy are the poor in spirit; theirs is the kingdom of heaven. Happy *the gentle; they shall have the earth for their heritage.* Happy those who mourn: they shall be comforted. Happy those who hunger and thirst for what is right: they shall be satisfied. Happy the merciful: they shall have mercy shown them. Happy the pure in heart: they shall see God. Happy the peacemakers: they shall be called sons of God. Happy those who are persecuted in the cause of right: theirs is the kingdom of heaven."

Matthew 6:14–15 Yes, if you forgive others their failings, your heavenly Father will forgive you yours; but if you do not forgive others, your Father will not forgive your failings either.

Luke 6:37 Do not judge, and you will not be judged yourselves; do not condemn, and you will not be condemned yourselves; grant pardon, and you will be pardoned.

Matthew 18:21–22 Then Peter went up to him and said, "Lord, how often must I forgive my brother if he wrongs me? As often as seven times?" Jesus answered, "Not seven, I tell you, but seventy-seven times."

Mark 11:25 And when you stand in prayer, forgive whatever you have against anybody, so that your Father in heaven may forgive your failings too.

Luke 11:4 . . . for we ourselves forgive each one who is in debt to us. And do not put us to the test.

Luke 17:3–4 Watch yourselves!
If your brother does something wrong, reprove him and, if he is sorry, forgive him. And if he wrongs you seven times a day and seven times comes back to you and says, "I am sorry," you must forgive him.

Matthew 5:44–48 But I say this to you: love your enemies and pray for those who persecute you; in this way you will be sons of your Father in heaven, for he causes his sun to rise on bad men as well as good, and his rain to fall on honest and dishonest men alike. For if you love those who love you, what right have you to claim any credit? Even the tax collectors do as much, do they not? And if you save your greetings for your brothers, are you doing anything exceptional? Even the pagans do as much, do they not? You must therefore be perfect just as your heavenly Father is perfect.

Luke 6:29–31 To the man who slaps you on one cheek, present the other cheek too; to the man who takes your cloak from you, do not refuse your tunic. Give to everyone who asks you, and do not ask for your property back from the man who robs you. Treat others as you would like them to treat you.

John 15:12 This is my commandment: love one another, as I have loved you.

Matthew 21:12–17 Jesus then went into the Temple and drove out all those who were selling and buying there; he upset the tables of the money changers and the chairs of those who were selling pigeons. "According to scripture," he said, *"my house will be called a house of prayer;* but you are turning it into a *robbers' den."* There were also blind and lame people who came to him in the Temple, and he cured them. At the sight of the wonderful things he did and of the children shouting, "Hosanna to the Son of David" in the Temple, the chief priests and the scribes were indignant. "Do you hear what they are saying?" they said to him. "Yes," Jesus answered, "have you never read this: *By the mouths of children, babes in arms, you have made sure of praise?"* With that he left them and went out of the city to Bethany where he spent the night.

John 3:13-25 "No one has gone up to heaven except the one who came down from heaven, the Son of Man who is in heaven; and the Son of Man must be lifted up as Moses lifted up the serpent in the desert, so that everyone who believes may have eternal life in him. Yes, God loved the world so much that he gave his only Son, so that everyone who believes in him may not be lost but may have eternal life. For God sent his Son into the world not to condemn the world, but so that through him the world might be saved. No one who believes in him will be condemned; but whoever refuses to believe is condemned already, because he has refused to believe in the name of God's only Son. On these grounds is sentence pronounced: that though the light has come into the world men have shown they prefer darkness to the light because their deeds were evil. And indeed, everybody who does wrong hates the light and avoids it, for fear his actions should be exposed; but the man who lives by the truth comes out into the light, so that it may be plainly seen that what he does is done in God."

After this, Jesus went with his disciples into the Judaean countryside and stayed with them there and baptised. At the same time John was baptising at Aenon near Salim, where there was plenty of water, and people were going there to be baptised. This was before John had been put in prison.

Now some of John's disciples had opened a discussion with a Jew about purification. . . .

Galatians 3:13 Christ redeemed us from the curse of the Law by being cursed for our sake, since scripture says: *Cursed be everyone who is hanged on a tree.*

Luke 23:34 Jesus said, "Father, forgive them; they do not know what they are doing." Then they cast lots to share out his clothing.

Romans 8:36-39 As scripture promised: *For your sake we are being massacred daily, and reckoned as sheep for the slaughter.* These are the trials through which we triumph, by the power of him who loved us.

For I am certain of this: neither death nor life, no angel, no prince, nothing that exists, nothing still to come, not any power, or height or depth, nor any created thing, can ever come between us and the love of God made visible in Christ Jesus our Lord.

John 14:27 Peace I bequeath to you, my own peace I give you, a peace the world cannot give, this is my gift to you. Do not let your hearts be troubled or afraid.

Romans 5:1-2 So far then we have seen that, through our Lord Jesus Christ, by faith we are judged righteous and at peace with God, since it is by faith and through Jesus that we have entered this state of grace in which we can boast about looking forward to God's glory.

Colossians 1:20 . . . and all things to be reconciled through him and for him, everything in heaven and everything on earth, when he made peace by his death on the cross.

Ephesians 2:13-22 But now in Christ Jesus, you that used to be so far apart from us have been brought very close, by the blood of Christ. For he is the peace between us, and has made the two into one and broken down the barrier which used to keep them apart, actually destroying in his own person the hostility caused by the rules and decrees of the Law. This was to create one single New

Man in himself out of the two of them and by restoring peace through the cross, to unite them both in a single Body and reconcile them with God. In his own person he killed the hostility. Later he came to bring the good news of peace, *peace to you who were far away and peace to those who were near at hand.* Through him, both of us have in the one Spirit our way to come to the Father.

So you are no longer aliens or foreign visitors: you are citizens like all the saints, and part of God's household. You are part of a building that has the apostles and prophets for its foundations, and Christ Jesus himself for its main cornerstone. As every structure is aligned on him, all grow into one holy temple in the Lord; and you too, in him, are being built into a house where God lives, in the Spirit.

Galatians 3:28 . . . and there are no more distinctions between Jew and Greek, slave and free, male and female, but all of you are one in Christ Jesus.

John 20:19–29 In the evening of that same day, the first day of the week, the doors were closed in the room where the disciples were, for fear of the Jews. Jesus came and stood among them. He said to them, "Peace be with you," and showed them his hands and his side. The disciples were filled with joy when they saw the Lord, and he said to them again, "Peace be with you. As the Father sent me, so am I sending you." After saying this he breathed on them and said: "Receive the Holy Spirit. For those whose sins you forgive, they are forgiven; for those whose sins you retain, they are retained."

Thomas, called the Twin, who was one of the Twelve, was not with them when Jesus came. When the disciples said, "We have seen the Lord," he answered, "Unless I see the holes that the nails made in his hands and can put my finger into the holes they made, and unless I can put my hand into his side, I refuse to believe." Eight days later the disciples were in the house again and Thomas was with them. The doors were closed, but Jesus came in and stood among them. "Peace be with you," he said. Then he spoke to Thomas, "Put your finger here; look, here are my hands. Give me your hand; put it into my side. Doubt no longer but believe." Thomas replied, "My Lord and my God!" Jesus said to him: "You believe because you can see me. Happy are those who have not seen and yet believe."

2 Corinthians 5:19-20 In other words, God in Christ was reconciling the world to himself, not holding men's faults against them, and he has entrusted to us the news that they are reconciled. So we are ambassadors for Christ; it is as though God were appealing through us, and the appeal that we make in Christ's name is: be reconciled to God.

Matthew 28:16-20 Meanwhile the eleven disciples set out for Galilee, to the mountain where Jesus had arranged to meet them. When they saw him they fell down before him, though some hesitated. Jesus came up and spoke to them. He said, "All authority in heaven and on earth has been given to me. Go, therefore, make disciples of all the nations; baptise them in the name of the Father and of the Son and of the Holy Spirit, and teach them to observe all the commands I gave you. And know that I am with you always; yes, to the end of time."

Luke 24:44-53 Then he told them, "This is what I meant when I said, while I was still with you, that everything written about me in the Law of Moses, in the Prophets and in the Psalms, has to be fulfilled." He then opened their minds to understand the scriptures, and he said to them, "So you see how it is written that the Christ would suffer and on the third day rise from the dead, and that, in his name, repentance for the forgiveness of sins would be preached to all the nations, beginning from Jerusalem. You are witnesses to this.

"And now I am sending down to you what the Father has promised. Stay in the city then, until you are clothed with the power from on high."

Then he took them out as far as the outskirts of Bethany, and lifting up his hands he blessed them. Now as he blessed them, he withdrew from them and was carried up to heaven. They worshipped him and then went back to Jerusalem full of joy; and they were continually in the Temple praising God.

Ephesians 1:9-10 He has let us know the mystery of his purpose . . . that he would bring everything together under Christ, as head, everything in the heavens and everything on earth.

Session 5
Peace Is Possible

Assignment: Have the students read from the NCCB pastoral letter (nos. 56–79). Ask the students to answer, in writing, the following questions:

1) According to the bishops' statement the tension between the vision of the reign of God and its concrete realization in history is often described in terms of "already but not yet." What do the bishops mean by "already but not yet" (no. 58)?

2) Why do the bishops say, "Peace is rightly and appropriately called an 'enterprise of justice' " (Isaiah 32:7) (no. 68).

Teaching Goal: To help students keep alive the hope and conviction that peace is possible.

Session Objective: For the students to share with one another their views on the possibility of peace in the world today and for them to identify the conviction that peace is possible expressed by the Catholic bishops of the United States in their pastoral letter.

Revised Objective:

Class Activity:

Have two students read aloud for the class "An Interview with Billy" (in format for duplication, at the end of this session), one taking the part of Melanie and one Billy. Then ask the students to discuss: Do you think Billy really believes peace is possible? Why or why not? Do *you* think peace is possible? Why or why not? What do the bishops mean by the phrase "already but not yet"? Why do the bishops say, "Peace is rightly and appropriately called an 'enterprise of justice' "? (30 minutes)

Summary: Highlight key points from the discussion. Write on the board the following points and elaborate on each:

* *Peace must be constructed on the basis of central human values: truth, justice, freedom, and love* (no. 68).
* *Peace is possible but never assured* (no. 60).
* *Justice is always the foundation of peace* (no. 60).

(15–20 minutes)

AN INTERVIEW WITH BILLY

Melanie: *Have you always lived in this neighborhood?*

Billy: My family has been here twenty years, and I have been here since 1968—thirteen years.

Do you think about leaving here someday?
Yeh, after I graduate from high school, I think about going and living in the wilderness. I don't know if I'll be happy there; I am so used to living in the city.

Do you think about what kind of work you'd like to do?
I'm interested in making greeting cards. Instead of going out and buying cards for Christmas, I make my own. I'm into writing stuff like that. Sometimes I'd like to have a job where I could eliminate things that aren't needed, like some things that happen in school. But my only goal for a job is writing greeting cards.

How old will you be in the year 2000?
Thirty-one.

Can you imagine the year 2000?
No.

Why not?
I don't know. I don't think much into the future. I see life as a day-to-day process. With everything that is going on in this world, someone could push a button and it would all be over. [Billy makes the motion of pushing a button and then makes the sound of a big explosion.]

How could that happen?
Nuclear arms and the government going crazy. They've got so much power.

Who could push the button? Do you think this country could do that?

Yeh, well, it depends on who's in the government. If they are greedy and go after another country or something. I see no reason for stuff like that, I mean going after another country. But I usually don't think into the future.

Does the thought of someone pushing that button scare you?
Sometimes, like when I think I want to do something with the future years and then I think, "Maybe there isn't going to be tomorrow." So, I don't get my hopes up too high.

So it is hard for you to imagine yourself being thirty-one years old?
Well, I could imagine it, but I also have this thought in my mind that there might not be tomorrow, or the next 10 minutes or something.

Billy, I have a fantasy question. Let's say you get a call tonight from the White House. Likely situation, right?
Yeh, happens all the time.

So, you get this call from President Reagan and he tells you he is sitting in the Oval Office waiting to talk with you, and you have this one chance to tell him what you think.
About what?

About anything at all, anything that you think is important. What would it be?
Probably about nuclear arms and nuclear material. They are getting some weirdo thoughts about putting nuclear waste in Lake Erie. Wouldn't that be wonderful? In our water supply? I'd tell him stuff like that.

What would you want him to do?
Not use the arms and have him realize all the people whose lives he is jeop . . . jeop . . .

Jeopardizing?
Yeh, my language is not so good tonight.

Excerpted from "How Old Will You Be in the Year 2000?" by Melanie Morrison in the July–August 1982 issue of *Sojourners,* pp. 16–19. Reprinted with permission from *Sojourners,* P.O. Box 29272, Washington, D.C. 20017.

I think it's fine. Okay, let's pretend Ronald Reagan says to you, "Billy, that is a nice thought. I would like to have disarmament just as you would, but what about the Soviets? They have lots of nuclear weapons, so we have to have lots also." What would you say then, Billy?

I'd say, "Work it out with the Russians, Mr. Reagan. We had the SALT Treaty going but we didn't deal with it, so they think you want war so they are going to keep building up their weapons. But, maybe if you show them that we are willing to let down some of our weapons, they will start letting down some of their weapons." That's what I'd say.

How do you know about things like the SALT Treaty?

From CBS News.

Do you think disarmament is possible?

Yes, peace is possible.

So the world doesn't have to explode tomorrow?

No, it doesn't have to explode for a couple more million years until the sun causes it to explode.

If it doesn't have to explode and if disarmament is possible, then why does the arms race keep going?

Because those in government think that the other ones are going to outnumber them and they want to be the most powerful. Until people change their minds about that, it's going to keep on going. There is not much you can do about it. If someone gets in office and they decide that they don't like the Russians and they want to blow them to pieces the next day, there isn't much you can do about it.

Do you have times when the thought of a nuclear war just comes crashing in?

I usually don't think about it when I'm doing something. But when I am sitting down by myself, I start thinking about it.

What do you think you'd do if that moment really happens?

I'd probably start praying, because there isn't much else you can do.

You don't believe fallout shelters can protect you?

No, because when it hits, the radiation will start spreading out all over the place causing diseases that the doctors have never even heard of and you'd have like six months to live.

Why is it then that people in the government are talking about fighting a "limited" nuclear war?

I wonder about that too, because we are still using violence. Someone says, "Well, we won't kill as many people with this MX bomb as with this other one." But we are still taking someone's life, and one life is worth as much as 10 million lives.

Do you think killing is ever justified?

No.

When you turn eighteen will you register with the Selective Service?
No.

Would you ever participate in war?
No.

Even if this country were invaded?
No.

Do you think this country could be in a war, say, within the next five or ten years?
If people have the attitudes they do now about this kind of stuff, yeh, it could happen.

Do you find that people your age talk about this sort of thing—about the arms race, for example?
Some people. Most of the kids don't really care.

Does this bother you?

In a way, yeh, because this is going to be their future if there is anything.

Are there some people with whom you can talk about these things?
Yeh, but most of them don't get interested because they think it is going to happen just like that [Billy snaps his fingers] and they don't think there is anything they can do about it. Or they get disappointed because they didn't change things overnight by writing some letter to the government or something.

You said before that peace is possible. Do you feel hopeful?
Yeh, I think there is hope for peace, but until then we have to live with the fear of being blown into oblivious.

Oblivion?
Yeh.

Session 6
The Just-War Theory

Assignment: Have the students read the NCCB pastoral letter (nos. 80-121). Ask the students to express their agreement or disagreement with the following statement and to be prepared to explain reasons for the stand they take.

The pacifist option and nonviolent tradition can be described as a gospel ideal rooted in early Church traditions and can be a realistic alternative to the just-war theory.

☐ agree   ☐ disagree

Why?

Teaching Goal: To help the students understand the Christian perspective on the just-war theory and on the pacifist option and nonviolent traditions.

Session Objective: For the students to identify the seven conditions required for the just-war theory and to reflect on the support the Catholic bishops of the United States give to the pacifist option and nonviolent witness as a means to peace.

Revised Objective:

Class Activities:

1) Review with the students the just-war theory (nos. 80–110) as discussed in the bishops' pastoral letter. On the board list the seven conditions explained:

- *just cause*
- *competent authority*
- *comparative justice*
- *right intention*
- *last resort*
- *probability of success*
- *proportionality*

Discuss with the students: Could a nuclear war ever be justified? If so, how? If not, why not? (20 minutes)

2) Review with the students the value of nonviolence as it is described in the bishops' pastoral (nos. 111–121).

In reference to the assignment for this session, determine how many students agree and how many disagree with the statement:

The pacifist option and nonviolent tradition can be described as a gospel ideal rooted in early Church traditions and can be a realistic alternative to the just-war theory.

Invite the students to discuss why they agree or disagree with the above statement. (20 minutes)

Summary: Ask the students to imagine that a powerful, dictatorial group of invaders has taken over the school. They are replacing the teachers and are making all the rules for the school. All student privileges are denied; strict and blind obedience is demanded of the students at all times. Ask the students: How would they react if they were committed to the pacifist option? to nonviolent resistance? to militant control? Ask the students: Which one of the above options they would choose? Why? (10–15 minutes)

Session 7
The Bishops Take a Stand

Assignment: Have the students read from the NCCB pastoral letter (nos. 122–161). Then ask each student to interview five different people (parent, teacher, friend, stranger, etc.) and to record whether each person interviewed agrees or disagrees with the following statements:

1) We possess a power [nuclear weapons] which should never be used (no. 124).
   agree _____   disagree _____

2) Nuclear weapons might be used if we do not reverse our direction (no. 124).
   agree _____   disagree _____

3) The arms race is to be condemned as a danger, an act of aggression against the poor (no. 128).
   agree _____   disagree _____

4) The arms race is a folly which does not provide the security it promises (no. 128).
   agree _____   disagree _____

5) As a people we must refuse to legitimate the idea of nuclear war (no. 131).
   agree _____   disagree _____

6) We must reject nuclear war because rejection has been declared a moral imperative by the bishops of the United States (no. 132).
   agree _____   disagree _____

7) The dangerous and delicate nuclear relationship the superpowers now maintain should not exist (no. 133).
   agree _____   disagree _____

8) Nuclear warfare is a system which threatens mutual suicide, psychological damage to ordinary people, and economic distortion of priorities (no. 134).
   agree _____   disagree _____

9) Our "no" to nuclear war must, in the end, be definitive and decisive (no. 138).
   agree _____   disagree _____

10) The Catholic bishops of the United States see their role as moral teachers precisely in terms of helping to form public opinion with a clear determination to resist resort to nuclear war as an instrument of national policy. Such is a fitting and proper role for our bishops (no. 139).
   agree _____   disagree _____

11) There should be clear public resistance to the rhetoric of "winnable" nuclear wars, unrealistic expectations of "surviving" nuclear exchanges, and strategies of "protracted nuclear war" (no. 140).
   agree _____   disagree _____

12) The Catholic bishops of the United States seek to encourage a public attitude which sets stringent limits on the kind of actions our government and other governments will take on nuclear policy. This is a pastoral responsibility of our bishops (no. 141).
   agree _____   disagree _____

13) No Christian can rightfully carry out orders or policies deliberately aimed at killing noncombatants (no. 148).
   agree _____   disagree _____

14) We do not perceive any situation in which the deliberate initiation of nuclear warfare, on however restricted a scale, can be morally justified (no. 150).
   agree _____   disagree _____

15) The first imperative is to prevent any use of nuclear weapons and our hope is that leaders will resist the notion that nuclear conflict can be limited, contained, or won in any traditional sense (no. 161).
   agree _____   disagree _____

(*Note:* This assignment activity is available, in format for duplication, at the end of this session.)

Teaching Goal: To help the students address the buildup of nuclear weapons as a moral issue.

Session Objective: For the students to identify what the National Conference of Catholic Bishops is saying in regard to nuclear weapons.

Revised Objective:

Class Activities:

1) Have the students themselves complete the same interview survey they used for their assignment interviewing five other people. Then write on the board:

	AGREE		DISAGREE	
	student	other	student	other
1.				
2.				
3.				
4.				
5.				
6.				
7.				
8.				
9.				
10.				
11.				
12.				
13.				
14.				
15.				

Record for each statement the total number of students and of others interviewed that agree and that disagree with each statement. You can do this quickly by asking for a show of hands from the students indicating agreement or disagreement among the students themselves, and then ask each student to report his or her final tallies for the other people interviewed (for example—number 1: 3 agree, 2 disagree). Review with the students each of the fifteen statements and note the number of students and other people interviewed who agree and the number who disagree. (20 minutes)

2) Discuss with the students: (*a*) Did the people interviewed for the assignment given above know that all fifteen statements were based on passages in the pastoral letter? (*b*) How do you feel about the Catholic bishops' publicly making such statements? (*c*) In referring to the use of nuclear weapons, why do the bishops conclude that *prevention is our only recourse*? (20 minutes)

Summary: Choose a student to act as a reporter. Ask the students to imagine that they are the bishops of the United States. The reporter is looking for statements by the bishops to be aired on the national news. Have the reporter go around the room asking for definite statements from the bishops regarding

nuclear weapons. The statements in the assignment for this session are good examples. You might want to tape the reporter's interviews and then play the tape for the class, taking time to comment on the significance of the statements made. (15 minutes)

Additional or Alternative Activities:

• Stage a radio or TV program. Ask students to assume the roles of different bishops and give each a particular statement to read. (Those from the assignment above as well as others from the text can be used.) Give the students time to practice reading their statements clearly and with the sense of a bishop's authority. Ask one student to serve as moderator for the program to introduce the "bishops" and to make appropriate comments about the statements made. A few commercials on extravagant or superfluous products can both enliven the presentation and, by way of contrast, underscore the seriousness of the bishops' statements.

Follow the reading of these statements with the discussion question: What are the bishops saying about nuclear weapons?

• Form debate teams and debate:
Limited nuclear war *is* possible today.
Limited nuclear war *is not* possible today.

• Divide the class into three groups giving each group one of the following questions. Ask each group to share among themselves the answers to their respective questions. Have each group report to the entire class giving a summary of their responses to the question discussed.

1) What is counter population warfare?
2) Why do the bishops say "it is morally unjustifiable to support a 'first use' policy"?
3) Would it be possible to have a "limited" nuclear war?

• Stage a mock TV talk show. Play the role of moderator yourself or ask a student who is perceptive and can follow up on comments and pursue issues with the "guests."

Discuss the three issues raised by the questions from the alternative activity directly above, using each group, in turn, as the guest speakers on your mock talk show. Question and challenge the group playing the role of guest speakers. Facilitate discussion and debate within the group and invite the audience (the rest of the class) to ask questions of the guest speakers. The following questions can be used to get the groups started:

1) *Counter Population Warfare:* (*a*) What is counter population warfare? (*b*) What is the Catholic Church's stand on counter population warfare? (*c*) What if another country strikes first?

2) *The Initiation of Nuclear War:* (*a*) Can you think of any situation in which the initiation of nuclear war can be justified? (*b*) What is your stand on "first use" policy? (*c*) What if we are attacked by nonnuclear means?

3) *Limited Nuclear War:* (*a*) Is there any such thing as "limited" nuclear war? (*b*) What questions do the bishops ask about "limited" nuclear war? (*c*) What must a debate on "limited" nuclear war address in addition to the size of weapons intended or the strategies projected?

A SURVEY ON THE ARMS RACE AND NUCLEAR WAR

Interview five different people (parent, teacher, friend, stranger, etc.). Record whether or not each person interviewed agrees or disagrees with the following statements:

1. We possess a power [nuclear weapons] which should never be used.
   agree ☐   disagree ☐

2. Nuclear weapons might be used if we do not reverse our direction.
   agree ☐   disagree ☐

3. The arms race is to be condemned as a danger, an act of aggression against the poor.
   agree ☐   disagree ☐

4. The arms race is a folly which does not provide the security it promises.
   agree ☐   disagree ☐

5. As a people we must refuse to legitimate the idea of nuclear war.
   agree ☐   disagree ☐

6. We must reject nuclear war because rejection has been declared a moral imperative by the bishops of the United States.
   agree ☐   disagree ☐

7. The dangerous and delicate nuclear relationship the superpowers now maintain should not exist.
   agree ☐   disagree ☐

8. Nuclear warfare is a system which threatens mutual suicide, psychological damage to ordinary people, and economic distortion of priorities.
   agree ☐   disagree ☐

9. Our "no" to nuclear war must, in the end, be definitive and decisive.
   agree ☐   disagree ☐

10. The Catholic bishops of the United States see their role as moral teachers precisely in terms of helping to form public opinion with a clear determination to resist resort to nuclear war as an instrument of national policy. Such is a fitting and proper role for our bishops.
    agree ☐   disagree ☐

11. There should be clear public resistance to the rhetoric of "winnable" nuclear wars, unrealistic expectations of "surviving" nuclear exchanges, and strategies of "protracted nuclear war."
    agree ☐   disagree ☐

12. The Catholic bishops of the United States seek to encourage a public attitude which sets stringent limits on the kind of actions our government and other governments will take on nuclear policy. This is a pastoral responsibility of our bishops.
    agree ☐   disagree ☐

13. No Christian can rightfully carry out orders or policies deliberately aimed at killing noncombatants.

   agree ☐   disagree ☐

14. We do not perceive any situation in which the deliberate initiation of nuclear warfare, on however restricted a scale, can be morally justified.

   agree ☐   disagree ☐

15. The first imperative is to prevent any use of nuclear weapons and our hope is that leaders will resist the notion that nuclear conflict can be limited, contained, or won in any traditional sense.

   agree ☐   disagree ☐

Session 8
Deterrence

Assignment: Have the students read from the pastoral letter (nos. 162–199). Ask the students to find and list all the comments made by the bishops in this section of the pastoral which support the following statements:

1) Any use of nuclear weapons (including nuclear deterrence) is morally unacceptable.
2) Nuclear deterrence is tolerated with a strictly conditioned moral acceptance.

Teaching Goal: To help the students address the moral dimensions of nuclear deterrence by identifying what the National Conference of Catholic Bishops is saying about the issue.

Session Objective: For students to debate the issue of the use of nuclear weapons for deterrence purposes.

Revised Objective:

Class Activities:

1) Ask the students: How is deterrence defined in the bishops' pastoral? (dissuasion of a potential adversary from initiating an attack or conflict, often by the threat of unacceptable retaliatory damage [no. 163])

Ask students who agree with the statement "Any use of nuclear weapons is morally unacceptable" to read aloud quotations from the bishops' pastoral which support this statement.

Ask students who agree with the statement "Nuclear deterrence is tolerated with a strictly conditioned moral acceptance" to read aloud quotations from the bishops' pastoral which support this statement. (15 minutes)

2) Divide the class into three groups. Form debate teams and stage a debate: group one debating "that any use of nuclear weapons is morally unacceptable," group two debating that "nuclear deterrence is tolerated with a strictly conditioned moral accep-

tance." Group three will serve as judges and will decide the winning team after the debate. (30 minutes)

Summary: Recall key points from the discussions. Highlight the historical evidence that deterrence has not, in fact, set in motion the process of disarmament. List on the board: *Moral questions about deterrence: (1) possession, (2) intention, (3) use on civilians, (4) prevention by buildup, (5) continued escalation.* (10 minutes)

Additional or Alternative Activities:

• Help the students to consider whether deterrence, even if based on balance, is acceptable as a long-term basis for peace. Do this by discussing the following related ideas:

1) The intention to use nuclear weapons would violate the principle of proportionality; targeting civilian populations would violate the principle of discrimination.
2) If deterrence fails, the human consequences would be catastrophic.
3) The political relationship among countries involved in deterrence would be one of distrust.
4) If deterrence fails, there would be no assurance of *any* limits being maintained.
5) Deterrence consumes vitally needed resources.

• Write on the board: *"As clearly unsatisfactory as the deterrence posture of the United States is from a moral point of view, use of nuclear weapons by any of the nuclear powers would be an even greater evil."*

Discuss with the students: What are the criteria for morally assessing the elements of deterrence strategy? (See nos. 167–187 of the pastoral letter.)

• Review with the students the proposals for the current United States deterrence posture that the bishops oppose. (See nos. 188–190 of the pastoral letter.)

Discuss with the students the recommendations the bishops make in support of the concept of "sufficiency" as an adequate deterrence. (See no. 191 of the pastoral letter.)

Session 9
The Promotion of Peace: Proposals and Policies

Assignment: Have the students read from the bishops' pastoral (nos. 200–233). Ask each student to give special attention to one of the following six sections of the bishops' pastoral and to answer the question raised for the section he or she was assigned.

1) Accelerated work for arms control, reduction, and disarmament (nos. 203–208): *Name three steps called for by the bishops to accelerate work for arms control.* (End development, end employment, reduce numbers of existing weapons.)

2) Continued insistence on efforts to minimize the risk of any war (nos. 209–214): *In what way do the bishops call for a reversal of the present United States course regarding arms?* (The United States should renew efforts to develop multilateral controls on arms exports and should in this case also be willing to take carefully chosen independent initiatives to restrain the arms trade. Such steps would be particularly appropriate where the receiving government faces charges of gross and systematic human rights violations.)

3) The relationship of nuclear and conventional defenses (nos. 215–219): *What measures do the bishops claim are necessary if any program directed at reducing reliance on nuclear weapons is to succeed?* (Measures to reduce tensions and to work for the balanced reduction of conventional forces.)

4) Civil defense (no. 220): *Why have existing programs for civil defense against nuclear attack led to public skepticism and even ridicule and cast doubt on the credibility of the government?* (It is unclear in the public mind whether these [programs] are intended to offer significant protection against at least some forms of nuclear attack or are being put into place to enhance the credibility of the strategic deterrent forces by demonstrating an ability to survive an attack.)

5) Efforts to develop nonviolent means of conflict resolution (nos. 221–230): *Why do nonviolent means of resistance to evil deserve study and consideration?* (Nonviolence is not the way of the weak, the cowardly or the impatient. Citizens would be trained in the techniques of peaceable noncompliance and noncooperation as a means of hindering an invading force or nondemocratic government from imposing its will.)

6) The role of conscience (nos. 231–233): *What stand do the bishops take relative to the issue of conscientious objection?* (Insist upon respect for and legislative protection of the rights of both conscientious objection in general and for selective conscientious objection to participation in a particular war, either because of the ends being pursued or the means being used.)

Teaching Goal: To show the students how the positive vision of peace contained in Catholic teaching provides direction for policy and personal choices.

Session Objective: To introduce the students to specific steps proposed by the bishops that are aimed at a more adequate policy for preserving the peace in a nuclear age.

Revised Objective:

Class Activities:

1) Divide the class into six groups, one for each of the assignment questions. Have each group share among themselves their responses to the question asked of them. Also have each group select a reporter and prepare a report for the entire class. The report should include an answer to the question asked and should suggest several things students can do to be involved in and to help promote the steps proposed for reducing the danger of war. (15 minutes)

2) Have each group report to the class, clearly answering the question assigned, and ask each group to list on the board one or two specific things students can do in promoting steps for reducing the danger of war. (30 minutes)

Summary: Review with the students the six steps

recommended by the bishops and invite students to add to the list things they can do to be involved in and to promote these steps. If time permits ask the students to discuss and challenge some of the suggestions listed for student involvement. (15 minutes)

Additional or Alternative Activities:

• Divide the class into five groups and assign each group one of the five exercises given in the "United States Congress Exercise" (found, in format for duplication, at the end of this session). Each group is to imagine that it is a committee of the United States Congress. Ask the members of each group to share and to discuss within their group the resolutions they formulated for their assignment and then as a group to agree upon one well-stated resolution which they will present to the entire Congress (class) for debate. Their resolution should include a rationale. For example:

> *Whereas* not only should development and deployment of new weapons cease, the numbers of existing weapons must be reduced in a manner that reduces the danger of war; and *whereas* . . .
> *Be it resolved that* . . .

With the entire class playing the role of Congress, stage a legislative session of the United States Congress. Ask each group to present their resolution and carry on a debate or discussion with the entire class. Allow each group 20 to 25 minutes to discuss or debate the resolution and conclude the discussion or debate with a vote by the entire class.

Review with the students the outcome of the students' vote on each of the resolutions debated. Examine some of the *whereas* statements presented by the groups (committees) in order to highlight significant rationale statements on promoting steps to reduce the danger of war. Assuming you are in a situation which allows 50 or 60 minute sessions, this entire activity will take three sessions. If your time is limited you might have each group simply give a brief report and then have the class vote for the one resolution which will be brought before the Congress.

• Conscience Formation: How have your attitudes about war and peace, weapons, and negotiations, etc. been formed?

By way of introduction, remind the students that the Church affirms that conscience is the most secret core and sanctuary of a person. The Church highly respects the consciences of its believing members (*Gaudium et Spes*, no. 16 ff.). The Church also asserts that each Christian must develop a carefully informed conscience. The purpose of this activity is to more thoroughly inform and develop the individual conscience.

With the entire class brainstorm on the following questions, which are adapted from the *Reverence for Life and Family Program Manual* (Dubuque: Wm. C. Brown, 1981) by Rev. John E. Forliti of the Archdiocese of St. Paul and Minneapolis.

1) **Who or what affects the formation of our Christian values?** (These are otherwise known as *influences:* family; friends; the media—press, TV, magazines; society in general; Church teaching.)

Ask the students to give examples of how each of the above influences affects the formation of Christian values. Then pick several statements from the resolutions formulated by the students for the first alternative activity above, and ask the students to give examples of how the five influences listed above helped form the attitudes they hold. (If the first alternative assignment was not used, ask students to volunteer a few values they strongly believe in and have them give examples of how the five influences listed above helped shape these attitudes or values in their lives.)

2) **What are the main sources that shape our Christian values?** (*Sources* of our Christian values: Scripture, the commandments, Jesus as model; Church teaching; liturgy and sacraments; faith experiences—e.g., love, forgiveness, sharing, etc.; other persons as Christian models.)

Ask the students to explain how these are sources of our Christian values.

Clarify the influences on the sources of Christian value formation. Our Christian conscience is developed only to the degree that we allow these influences and sources to touch our lives. It may be helpful to close with a scriptural reading that exemplifies the role of Jesus and Scripture in the formation of conscience. Suggested scriptural passages: Luke 6:43–49; Luke 4:1–13; Matthew 5:3–10; Isaiah 42:1–3.

36

UNITED STATES CONGRESS EXERCISE

1. Accelerated Work for Arms Control, Reduction, and Disarmament

Imagine that you are a member of a committee of the United States Congress. Your committee is charged to bring to the floor a proposal on "Accelerated Work for Arms Control, Reduction, and Disarmament." For your committee work you are to read a section (nos. 203–208) of the NCCB pastoral letter, *The Challenge of Peace: God's Promise and Our Response,* and to formulate a resolution which will be presented to the committee. Your resolution should reflect the recommendations of the bishops. In addition, give a rationale for your resolution by composing several **whereas statements** that explain the reasons for your resolution. For example:

> **Whereas** not only should development and deployment of new weapons cease, the numbers of existing weapons must be reduced in a manner that reduces the danger of war;
>
> and **whereas** . . .
>
> **be it resolved that** . . .

2. Continued Insistence on Efforts to Minimize the Risk of Any War

Imagine that you are a member of a committee of the United States Congress. Your committee is charged to bring to the floor a proposal on "Continued Insistence on Efforts to Minimize the Risk of Any War." For your committee work you are to read a section (nos. 209–214) of the NCCB pastoral letter, *The Challenge of Peace: God's Promise and Our Response,* and to formulate a resolution which will be presented to the committee. Your resolution should reflect the recommendations of the bishops. In addition, give a rationale for your resolution by composing several **whereas statements** that explain the reasons for your resolution. For example:

> **Whereas** not only should development and deployment of new weapons cease, the numbers of existing weapons must be reduced in a manner that reduces the danger of war;
>
> and **whereas** . . .
>
> **be it resolved that** . . .

3. Efforts to Develop Nonviolent Means of Conflict Resolution

Imagine that you are a member of a committee of the United States Congress. Your committee is charged to bring to the floor a proposal on "Efforts to Develop Nonviolent Means of Conflict Resolution." For your committee work you are to read a section (nos. 221–230) of the NCCB pastoral letter, *The Challenge of Peace: God's Promise and Our Response,* and to formulate a resolution which will be presented to the committee. Your resolution should reflect the recommendations of the bishops. In addition, give a rationale for your resolution by composing several **whereas statements** that explain the reasons for your resolution. For example:

> **Whereas** not only should development and deployment of new weapons cease, the numbers of existing weapons must be reduced in a manner that reduces the danger of war;
>
> and **whereas** . . .
>
>
> **be it resolved that** . . .

4. The Role of Conscience

Imagine that you are a member of a committee of the United States Congress. Your committee is charged to bring to the floor a proposal on "The Role of Conscience." For your committee work you are to read a section (nos. 231–233) of the NCCB pastoral letter, *The Challenge of Peace: God's Promise and Our Response,* and to formulate a resolution which will be presented to the committee. Your resolution should reflect the recommendations of the bishops. In addition, give a rationale for your resolution by composing several **whereas statements** that explain the reasons for your resolution. For example:

> **Whereas** not only should development and deployment of new weapons cease, the numbers of existing weapons must be reduced in a manner that reduces the danger of war;
>
> and **whereas** . . .
>
>
> **be it resolved that** . . .

5. The Relationship of Nuclear and Conventional Defenses

Imagine that you are a member of a committee of the United States Congress. Your committee is charged to bring to the floor a proposal on "The Relationship of Nuclear and Conventional Defenses." For your committee work you are to read a section (nos. 215–220) of the NCCB pastoral letter, *The Challenge of Peace: God's Promise and Our Response,* and to formulate a resolution which will be presented to the committee. Your resolution should reflect the recommendations of the bishops. In addition, give a rationale for your resolution by composing several **whereas statements** that explain the reasons for your resolution. For example:

> **Whereas** not only should development and deployment of new weapons cease, the numbers of existing weapons must be reduced in a manner that reduces the danger of war;
>
> and **whereas** . . .
>
>
> **be it resolved that** . . .

Session 10
Shaping a Peaceful World

Assignment: Give each student one of the three sections from "Quotations from Church Documents," and have the students share the quotations in that section with an adult (parent, teacher, neighbor, college student, etc.). Ask the students to discuss with this adult his or her reaction to the quotations: Do you agree or disagree with these quotations? Do you believe that our bishops should be making these statements? Why or why not? (*Note:* This assignment activity, "Quotations from Church Documents," is available, in format for duplication, at the end of this session.)

Teaching Goal: To help the students recognize global interdependence as a key factor in shaping a peaceful world.

Session Objective: For students to identify how the NCCB in its pastoral letter recognizes that shaping a peaceful world is based on meeting security and welfare needs in vast sectors of the globe.

Revised Objective:

Class Activities:

1) Ask the students who used the first set of quotations from the assignment above to share insights and reactions from the interviews they conducted. Review and discuss the quotations with the class and have a student or several students read aloud "World Order in Catholic Teaching" (nos. 234–244) from the NCCB pastoral letter. (15–20 minutes)

2) Ask students who used the second set of quotations from the assignment above to share insights and reactions from the interviews they conducted. Review and discuss the quotations with the class and have a student or several students read aloud "The Superpowers in a Disordered World" (nos. 245–258) from the NCCB pastoral letter. (15–20 minutes)

3) Ask the students who used the third set of quotations from the assignment above to share insights and reactions from the interviews they conducted. Review and discuss the quotations with the class and have a student or several students read aloud "Interdependence: From Fact to Policy" (nos. 259–273) from the NCCB pastoral letter. (15–20 minutes)

Summary: Write on the board: *Shaping a Peaceful World.* Then comment on the potential for each of the following to help shape a peaceful world: (*a*) moral bonds of rights and duties, (*b*) moral interdependence, (*c*) material interdependence, (*d*) security, welfare, safety. (5–10 minutes)

Additional or Alternative Activity:

Use the film *Dietrich Bonhoeffer: Memories and Perspectives,* available in an edited video version. This 60-minute version was made especially with the classroom in mind. It is largely dialogue and would be most effective used with highly motivated and older students.

The film presents the biography of a young German Protestant theologian, Dietrich Bonhoeffer, who led the Christian resistance movement against Hitler. He was executed only a few days before liberation in 1945. The film was developed from archival film, home movies, private photos, and oral history given by relatives, friends, and disciples.

This edited video version can be purchased for $295.00. (You might want to network with two or three other institutions to share the cost and make the film available to a larger number of people in your area.) A 90-minute version is available for rental for $95.00. Write to: Trinity Films, Inc., 2524 Hennepin Avenue, Minneapolis, MN 55405.

QUOTATIONS FROM CHURCH DOCUMENTS

A. World Order in Catholic Teaching

1. "Peace cannot be limited to a mere absence of war, the result of an ever precarious balance of forces. No, peace is something built up day after day, in the pursuit of an order intended by God, which implies a more perfect form of justice among men and women." (Paul VI, *The Development of Peoples*, 1966, no. 76)

2. "The fundamental premise of world order in Catholic teaching is a theological truth: the unity of the human family—rooted in common creation, destined for the kingdom and united by moral bonds of rights and duties." (*The Challenge of Peace*, no. 236)

3. ". . . one of the primary functions of Catholic teaching on world order has been to point the way toward a more integrated international system." (*The Challenge of Peace*, no. 239)

4. "An important element missing from world order today is a properly constituted political authority with the capacity to shape our material interdependence in the direction of moral interdependence." (*The Challenge of Peace*, no. 241)

5. "Justice, right reason and humanity, therefore, urgently demand that the arms race should cease; that the stockpiles which exist in various countries should be reduced equally and simultaneously by the parties concerned; that nuclear weapons should be banned; and that a general agreement should eventually be reached about progressive disarmament and an effective method of control." (John XXIII, *Peace on Earth*, 1963, no. 112)

B. The Superpowers in a Disordered World

1. "Peace cannot be limited to a mere absence of war, the result of an ever precarious balance of forces. No, peace is something built up day after day, in the pursuit of an order intended by God, which implies a more perfect form of justice among men and women." (Paul VI, *The Development of Peoples*, 1966, no. 76)

2. "The diplomatic requirement for addressing the U.S.-Soviet relationship is not romantic idealism about Soviet intentions and capabilities but solid realism which recognizes that everyone will lose in a nuclear exchange." (*The Challenge of Peace,* no. 257)

3. "To believe we are condemned in the future only to what has been the past of U.S.-Soviet relations is to underestimate both our human potential for creative diplomacy and God's action in our midst which can open the way to changes we could barely imagine." (*The Challenge of Peace,* no. 258)

4. "All must realize that there is no hope of putting an end to the building up of armaments, nor of reducing the present stocks, nor still less of abolishing them altogether unless the process is complete and thorough and unless it proceeds from inner conviction; unless, that is, everyone sincerely co-operates to banish the fear and anxious expectations of war with which [people] are oppressed. If this is to come about, the fundamental principle on which our present peace depends must be replaced by another, which declares that the true and solid peace of nations can consist, not in equality of arms, but in mutual trust alone." (John XXIII, *Peace on Earth*, 1963, no. 113)

C. Interdependence: From Fact to Policy

1. "Peace cannot be limited to a mere absence of war, the result of an ever precarious balance of forces. No, peace is something built up day after day, in the pursuit of an order intended by God, which implies a more perfect form of justice among men and women." (Paul VI, *The Development of Peoples*, 1966, no. 76)

2. "The numerous U.N. studies on the relationship of development and disarmament support the judgment of Vatican II . . . 'The arms race is one of the greatest curses on the human race and the harm it inflicts upon the poor is more than can be endured.'" (*The Challenge of Peace*, no. 269)

3. "In an interdependent world, the security of one nation is related to the security of all. When we consider how and what we pay for defense today, we need a broader view than the equation of arms with security." (*The Challenge of Peace*, no. 270)

4. "If the arms race in all its dimensions is not reversed, resources will not be available for the human needs so evident in many parts of the globe and in our own country as well." (*The Challenge of Peace*, no. 271)

5. "The moral challenge of interdependence concerns shaping the relationships and rules of practice which will support our common need for security, welfare, and safety." (*The Challenge of Peace*, no. 273)

6. ". . . it is with deep sorrow that we note the enormous stocks of armaments that have been and still are being made in the more economically developed countries with a vast outlay of intellectual and economic resources. And so it happens that, while the people of these countries are loaded with heavy burdens, other countries as a result are deprived of the collaboration they need in order to make economic and social progress." (John XXIII, *Peace on Earth*, 1963, no. 109)

Session 11
Challenge and Response

Assignment: Have the students read from the NCCB pastoral letter, "The Church: A Community of Conscience, Prayer and Penance" (nos. 274–278) and "Elements of a Pastoral Response" (nos. 279–300). Ask the students to answer, in writing, the following questions: (1) A response to the call of Jesus is both personal and demanding. To be a disciple of Jesus requires that we continually go beyond where we are now. In what way has this unit on the bishops' pastoral letter helped you to become a disciple of Jesus (going beyond where you are now)? (2) Why is war taken for granted in so many parts of the world today? (3) What do the bishops say are the many faces of violence in today's society? (4) Why is prayer and penance such an essential part of our efforts to shape a peaceful world?

Teaching Goal: To raise options for individual and group actions intended to help create a world of peace and understanding.

Session Objective: For students to identify and reflect on ways they can respond to the challenge of peace in this nuclear age.

Revised Objective:

Class Activities:

1) Review and discuss with the students their responses to the questions asked in the assignment above. (15 minutes)

2) Use the film *Gods of Metal* (Maryknoll Films, Maryknoll, NY 10545; $25.00 rental, $325.00 purchase). This is a 27–minute documentary about the nuclear arms race and some of those who are trying to stop it. The film shows what individuals and groups are doing to halt the arms buildup and gives practical suggestions on what each of us can do to help create a world of peace and understanding. (30 minutes)

Summary: Ask the students to react to the film and to share ideas they may have gotten for ways they can respond to the challenge of peace in a nuclear age. (10 minutes)

Session 12
Challenge and Hope

Assignment: Have the students read "Challenge and Hope" (nos. 301–329) from the NCCB pastoral letter. Ask each student to imagine that he or she is living one of the following lifestyles or careers:

- a priest
- a religious (brother or sister)
- a teacher
- a parent
- a teenager
- a military person
- a person in defense industries
- a scientist
- a TV and/or newspaper reporter
- a public official
- a Catholic citizen

Ask the students to study the section of the NCCB pastoral letter which is addressed to the lifestyle or career he or she is to imagine living, and have the students write a letter to a friend explaining how the bishops are challenging him or her to work with them in helping to share a peaceful world.

Teaching Goal: To help the students recognize the challenge the bishops are presenting in this pastoral letter.

Session Objective: For students to identify options for responding to the challenge of this pastoral letter.

Revised Objective:

Class Activities:

1) Divide the class into eleven groups according to the eleven lifestyle or career categories listed in the assignment. (There will likely be two or three students to a group.) Have each group share among themselves the letters they wrote for their assignment. Then, have each group list and discuss one or two ways in which a person with that particular lifestyle or career could help to shape a peaceful world. (15 minutes)

2) Ask each group to report to the entire class, simply stating the lifestyle or career involved, the challenge the bishops are presenting, and one or two ways a person with that lifestyle or career could help to shape a peaceful world. (15 minutes)

3) Read and discuss with the students the "Conclusion" (nos. 330–339) of the pastoral. (10 minutes)

Summary: Conclude the session with a group prayer. See, for example, the prayer service (formatted for duplication) beginning on the following page.

PRAYER SERVICE

Leader: Let us remember that we are in God's presence. Peace is a gift from God. We will be able to make that gift come alive in the world only if our vision is enlightened by Wisdom. Our efforts must be strengthened and shaped by God's saving grace. Through prayer we truly become instruments in the Lord's hands, instruments capable of establishing and maintaining peace.

[Divide the class into two groups to recite the prayer of Saint Francis of Assisi. Have the two groups recite the prayer alternating the phrases as numbered below. Allow time for a pause between each phrase.]

Group 1: Lord make me an instrument of Your peace.
Group 2: Where there is hatred, let me sow love.
    1: Where there is injury, pardon;
    2: Where there is doubt, faith;
    1: Where there is despair, hope;
    2: Where there is darkness, light;
    1: Where there is sadness, joy;
    2: O Divine Master, grant that I may seek not so much to be consoled as to console;
    1: To be understood as to understand;
    2: To be loved as to love;
    1: For it is in giving that we receive;
    2: It is in pardoning that we are pardoned; and
    1: It is in dying that we are born to Eternal Life.

[Pause for a brief time of reflection and/or to sing a peace song. A popular peace song listened to and reflected on might serve well here too.]

PETITIONS

Leader: Lord God, we come to you in our need; create in us an awareness of the large and seemingly irreversible crises we face today, and give us a sense of responsibility to be active forces of good.

Leader: Where there is a blatant nationalism,
All: let there be a global, universal concern;

Leader: Where there is war and armed conflict,
All: let there be negotiation;

Leader: Where there is stockpiling,
All: let there be disarmament;

Leader: Where people struggle for freedom,
All: let there be noninterference;

Leader: Where there is careless waste,
All: let there be a care to preserve the earth's resources;

Leader: Where there is abundance,
All: let there be a choice for a simple lifestyle and sharing;

Leader: Where there is angry protest,
All: let there be a balance of prayerful dependence on God;

Leader: Where there is selfish individualism,
All: let there be an openness to community;

Leader: Where there is racism,
All: let there be a hand reached out in understanding;

Leader: Where there is sin of injustice,
All: let there be confession, forgiveness, and conversion;

Leader: Where there is despair and fear because of the enormity of the problems,
All: let there be confidence in You and in our collective efforts.

[Allow some time for the students to express personal prayers or petitions.]

Reader: Is not this the sort of fast that pleases me,
to break unjust fetters
and undo the thongs of the yoke,
to let the oppressed go free
and break every yoke,
to share your bread with the hungry,
and shelter the homeless poor,
to clothe the person you see to be naked
and not turn from your own kin?
Then will your light shine like the dawn
and your wound be quickly healed over.
If you do away with the yoke,
the clenched fist, the wicked word,
if you give your bread to the hungry
and relief to the oppressed,
your light will rise in the darkness,
and your shadows become like noon. (Isaiah 58:6–8; 10)

All [peace greeting]: Lord Jesus Christ, you said to your apostles: I leave you peace, my peace I give you. Look not on our sins, but on the faith of your Church, and grant us the peace and unity of your Kingdom.

[Have the students exchange individual greetings of peace with one another.]

All: Lord, let us not so much be concerned to be cared for as to care; not so much to be materially secure as to know that we are loved by God; let us not look to be served, but to place ourselves at the service of others, whatever the cost to self-interest; for it is in loving that we, like Jesus, experience the fullness of what it means to be human. And it is in serving that we discover the healing power of life that will bring a new sense of hope to our world. Amen.

Leader: ". . . what we are to be in the future has not yet been revealed; all we know is, that when it is revealed we shall be like him because we shall see him as he really is." (1 John 3:2)

[Conclude with an appropriate song or say the Lord's Prayer together.]

Appendix
Study Guide for Adult Discussion or Seminar Groups on *The Challenge of Peace*

This adult study guide has been adapted with permission from a study guide prepared by Ted Snyder of the Office of Social Development of the Archdiocese of Saint Paul and Minneapolis (formerly the Office of Urban Affairs). This guide is intended to assist Catholics in identifying the major themes of the bishops' pastoral letter and in reflecting upon their significance to citizens of the United States. It has been produced to promote reflection, discussion, and debate.

This guide is keyed to each section of the pastoral letter, which includes an introduction, four major sections (with subheadings), and a conclusion. Each section contains a brief description of its content and several questions to help the reader reflect upon the content. It is intended to be used *with* the text of the pastoral letter, not as a substitute. The guide can be used for personal study or group discussion.

INTRODUCTION

Fear of nuclear war is real and growing. The bishops, as the teachers of the Church, express their obligation to call their community of faith to conscious moral choices about the possession and use of nuclear arms.

1) Do you agree with the statement that they as bishops, ministering in a superpower, have a special responsibility to call the Catholic community to shape a "conscious choice" in response to the threat posed by nuclear weapons to the future of creation?

2) To what extent do you agree or disagree with the bishops' belief that the world is at a moment of crisis? that hope is feasible in this time of supreme crisis and fear?

3) What authority do bishops have to produce pastoral letters on current moral issues?

I. PEACE IN THE MODERN WORLD: RELIGIOUS PERSPECTIVES AND PRINCIPLES

Catholic social teaching is a mix of scriptural, theological, and philosophical elements which has evolved into a unified moral perspective on social, political, and economic affairs. This draft reflects the bishops' effort to examine the issues of war and peace in our time from the perspective of Catholic social teaching. They have two purposes: (1) to help Catholics form their consciences and (2) to contribute to the national public policy debate on war and peace.

1) What is the purpose of Catholic social teaching? Can it add anything important to the public debate of social issues? What role do you have in this debate?

2) Does Catholic social teaching serve as a guide in your personal decision making? Explain.

3) What is the distinctive part the Church has to play in the search for peace in the world?

4) What other social issues have the bishops addressed in the past?

A. Peace and the Kingdom

In the Scriptures, peace has many dimensions. All of them reflect the achievement of union with God. Peace is found in fidelity to the covenant between God and God's people, characterized by justice and mercy. Jesus rooted peace in love, which was incarnated in his life and teaching.

1) What do you understand by the statement "Peace and war must always be seen in light of God's intervention in human affairs and our response to that intervention"?

2) How do you understand the difference between "peace" and "justice"?

3) Is your understanding of "peace" consistent with the ways "peace" is described in the bishops' pastoral letter?

B. Kingdom and History

The reign of the kingdom of God, a kingdom of peace and justice, has begun now, in our own time. Christians live in a time of tension between the vision of that kingdom of peace and justice and its realization in life today. This pilgrim existence faces people of good will with moral options which may differ one from the other.

1) To what extent do you agree that "peace is possible"?

2) Why is justice always the foundation of peace?

3) Do you think debate over the Christian response to the arms race is healthy or destructive for the Catholic Church?

4) Are there issues other than nuclear weapons over which Christians disagree in good faith?

C. The Moral Choices for the Kingdom

Two legitimate moral responses to unjust aggression exist for Christians: (1) nonviolence, or refusal to engage in war activities; and (2) a just war, based on acknowledgement that under certain circumstances resistance to evil may require a violent response. Both start with the assumption that we must love our enemy and that the "taking of even one human life is a prospect we should consider in fear and trembling." The conditions which have historically entered into just-war decision making are enumerated and explained.

1) Can the nonviolent tradition be an alternative to the just-war theory?

2) Has our nation ever engaged in a war wherein the conditions for the just-war theory were fulfilled? Has our nation ever engaged in a war wherein the conditions for the just-war theory were violated?

3) Would you support or encourage a member of your family to be a pacifist? a conscientious objector? Why or why not?

4) What are your personal reactions or convictions about the two Christian responses to war described in this section of the pastoral letter?

II. WAR AND PEACE IN THE MODERN WORLD: PROBLEMS AND PRINCIPLES

The age of nuclear arms and the prospect of their use raises profound questions about the moral traditions of the Church. The power of nuclear arms threatens the created order and the future existence of the human race: "the meaning of sin in its most graphic dimension."

The nuclear age challenges the Church to examine its moral tradition in relation to the unique dangers of nuclear warfare.

• In what specific ways does nuclear warfare challenge the Church to reexamine its moral traditions?

A. The New Movement

The popes have taken strong exception to past and prospective use of nuclear arms, as well as criticizing the arms race. A body of knowledge which indicates the disastrous aftermath of any nuclear exchange is being assembled and broadly discussed. Yet, we are caught in previously developed systems of nuclear deterrence in a world of independent nations. The political dilemma which we face strains our capacity for moral reasoning and action. Yet people's concerns about the arms race are growing.

1) To what extent do you agree or disagree with each of the fifteen pastoral-based statements (see session 7 of this manual) taken from this section of the pastoral letter?

2) Do you believe that the task outlined in this section of the pastoral letter is possible?

3) Do you agree with the statement: "Our arguments in this pastoral must be detailed and nuanced . . . ."? Why or why not?

4) Would you agree that a simple "no" to the possession and use of nuclear arms is the direction of the pastoral? Why or why not?

B. Religious Leadership and the Public Debate

Pope John Paul II has called for a peace constituency to make possible public policies which limit the actions of government in the development and use of nuclear arms. The bishops address four issues related to nuclear weapons policy: (1) use of nuclear weapons, (2) the policy of deterrence in principle and practice, (3) reduction of the danger of war, and (4) long-term measures of policy and diplomacy.

We live in a pluralistic society. Some understand the exercise of leadership by bishops, on public policy issues, to transgress our constitutional separation of church and state.

1) What is your understanding of separation of church and state?

2) How do you regard this pastoral letter relative to separation of church and state?

3) What are the limits of religion in public policy debates?

C. The Use of Nuclear Weapons

Using the principles of just-war conduct explained earlier, the bishops evaluate three circumstances of using nuclear warfare. Nuclear weapons may not be used against civilian population centers. Initiation of nuclear war, even on a limited basis, cannot be justified. The possibility of a limited nuclear war not escalating to generalized exchange is very doubtful. Even in retaliation, the probability of expansion of a limited war is so high, that the use of nuclear weapons involves an unacceptably high moral risk.

Three circumstances of nuclear warfare are evaluated: use on civilian targets, first use of nuclear weapons, and limited nuclear war.

1) Do you think there could ever be a "just" nuclear war? Why or why not?

2) What is your stand on a "first use" policy? What stand do the bishops take?

3) Do you think there could ever be a "limited" nuclear war? Why or why not?

D. Deterrence in Principle and Practice

Deterrence persuades adversaries that initiation of attack will result in an unacceptably high level of damage to themselves. In discussing nuclear war, deterrence rather than defense is the focus, because defense against nuclear attack is not possible. The moral issues of nuclear deterrence are five: (1) the possession of weapons of mass destruction; (2) the threat of intention to use them; (3) the willingness to use nuclear weapons on civilians; (4) the moral significance of deterrence through a strategy which could not be morally implemented; (5) the continued escalation of the nuclear arms race and its diversion of resources from other needs. Continued reliance upon the possession of nuclear arms to deter their use by our adversaries is justified only in the context of action toward arms control and multilateral disarmament. (*Note: The moral reasoning in this section is specific and detailed, and requires close attention to understand its significance.*)

1) Which of the following two statements would you stand behind if forced into a debate or a position on the issue?
- Any use of nuclear weapons (including nuclear deterrence) is morally unacceptable.
- Nuclear deterrence is tolerated with a strictly conditioned moral acceptance.

2) Give historical evidence that deterrence has not, in fact, set in motion the process of disarmament.

3) What moral questions about deterrence can be raised in regard to each of the following: possession, intention, use on civilians, prevention by buildup, continued escalation.

III. THE PROMOTION OF PEACE: PROPOSALS AND POLICIES

Peace is not just the absence of war.

- What does peace involve?

A. Specific Steps to Reduce the Danger of War

Six proposed actions are set forth: (1) acceleration of nuclear arms control; (2) continued work to reduce the risk of any war; (3) consideration of the possibility that a reevaluation of present security arrangements and conventional military forces may be necessitated by nuclear reductions; (4) attention to existing programs for and problems with civil defense; (5) development of nonviolent conflict resolution techniques and mechanisms; and (6) formation of personal conscience on public policy questions and service to the common good.

1) To what extent do you agree with the bishops' call for a reversal of the present United States course regarding arms?

2) Why do nonviolent means of resistance to evil deserve study and consideration?

3) How realistic are the steps to reduce the danger of war presented by the bishops?

4) What steps do you believe should be added to the ones described in the pastoral letter?

5) What actions on our part are necessary if these steps are to be implemented?

B. Shaping a Peaceful World

Interdependence, rooted in the common humanity of us all, is the basic underpinning for a moral world order in Catholic social teaching. A more integrated system of international relations is a goal enunciated by Catholic social teaching and indicated by the myriad international issues which we face. U.S.–Soviet relations, even under the present adverse circumstances, require conscious attention to arrive at agreement on those points on which we share a common concern. The relationship between disarmament and development is a crucial issue for relations among nations.

1) Do you agree with the pastoral letter's assessment of the USSR?

2) What role does each of the following play in the issue of relations among nations: (a) moral bonds of rights and duties; (b) moral interdependence; (c) material interdependence; (d) security, welfare, safety.

3) What role does the United Nations play in the issue of relations among nations?

4) How effective do you feel the United Nations has been in developing relations among nations?

IV. THE PASTORAL CHALLENGE AND RESPONSE

A. The Church . . . ;
B. Elements of a Pastoral Response

The discipleship of Jesus requires continuing growth in a world which is increasingly estranged from the values of the gospel. The threat of nuclear war demands a response from Christians. The Church's role in the nuclear debate is to explain the principles of its social teaching and apply those principles to the concrete situation we face. The question for peace is an outgrowth of reverence for life. As Christians, we seek through prayer and penance conversion from the violence in our own lives.

1) Why is war taken for granted in so many parts of the world today?
2) What are the many faces of violence in today's society?
3) Who is the Church? What should the role of Catholic social teaching be in the debate of the moral challenge of nuclear war?
4) What other issues of public policy in which the Church has been involved are affected by the issue of nuclear arms and the danger of war?
5) What is the relationship of prayer and penance to our response to the danger of nuclear war?

C. Challenge and Hope

American Catholics are called to a primary loyalty to the peace, justice, and security of the human family. "Our national goals and policies must be measured against that standard." Our past use of nuclear weapons must be repented if we are to develop a national will against future use of those weapons. Every Catholic plays some role in confronting the nuclear threat; every Catholic is confronted by questions of conscience stemming from the nuclear arms race, from one's state in life, profession, and/or citizenship.

1) Why is it necessary that we repent for our past use of nuclear weapons?
2) What impact does this pastoral letter have on your life? What contribution can you make to the aims of this pastoral letter from your particular situation?
3) What should be different in your parish because of this pastoral letter?
4) How can your parish and/or the universal Church assist you in dealing with this issue?

CONCLUSION

God respects human freedom and does not impose solutions to human problems. Rather, God's grace helps us to take responsibility for confronting them as we shape creation to the ways of the kingdom of God. The task before us is to subject the power of the nuclear age to human control and utilize it for human benefit. This activity is sustained by hope in the final triumph of good over evil and transformation of creations: "Behold, I make all things new" (Rev. 21:5).

1) What role does the presence of Christ play in your confronting the more challenging issues of life?
2) Does the description of faith in the conclusion of this pastoral letter accurately describe your experience of faith?